This book belongs to

....

....

Useful words

(in the order they appear in this book)

 camel

 crocodile

 hippo

 hyena

 iguana

 insect

 rhino

 rabbit

 leopard

 lion

Grey letters represent silent letters.

 monkey

 mongoose

 ostrich

 otter

 tiger

 tortoise

 koala

 kangaroo

 gorilla

 gnu

 peacock

 parrot

3

Letterland Zoo

Maire Buonocore

Clever Cat, Clever Cat,

How do you do?

What can you see in the

Letterland zoo?

Hairy Hat Man,

How do you do?

What can you see in the

Letterland zoo?

8

Impy Ink, Impy Ink,

How do you do?

What can you see in the

Letterland zoo?

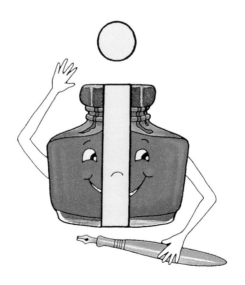

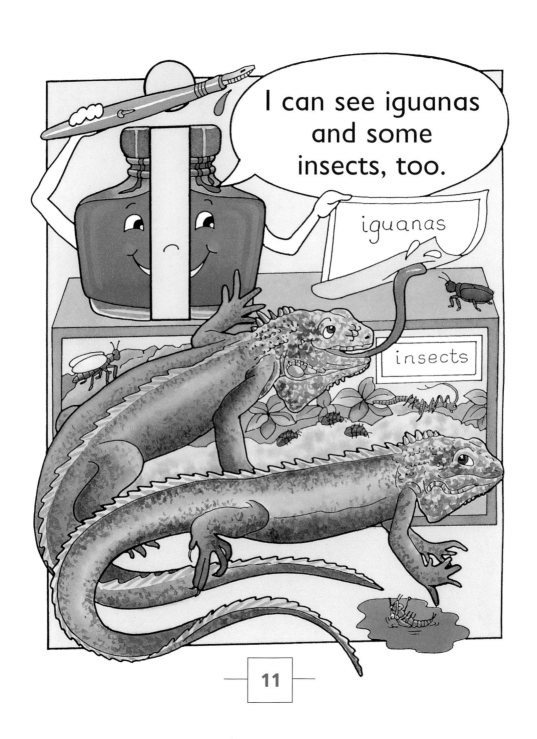

Robber Red, Robber Red,

How do you do?

What can you see in the

Letterland zoo?

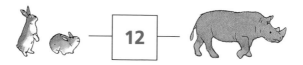

Lucy Lamp Lady,

How do you do?

What can you see in the

Letterland zoo?

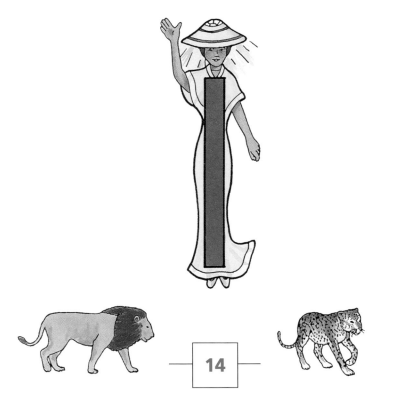

Munching Mike,

How do you do?

What can you see in the

Letterland zoo?

Oscar Orange,

How do you do?

What can you see in the

Letterland zoo?

Ticking Tess, Ticking Tess,

How do you do?

What can you see in the

Letterland zoo?

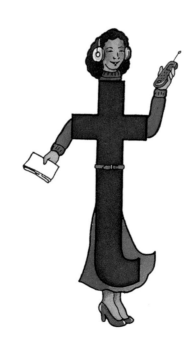

Kicking King, Kicking King,

How do you do?

What can you see in the

Letterland zoo?

Golden Girl, Golden Girl,

How do you do?

What can you see in the

Letterland zoo?

Poor Peter, Poor Peter,

How do you do?

What can you see in the

Letterland zoo?

Zig Zag Zebra,

How do you do?

What can you see in the

Letterland zoo?

The Letterlanders

Annie Apple	Bouncy Ben	Clever Cat	Dippy Duck	Eddy Elephant	Fireman Fred	Golden Girl

Hairy Hat Man	Impy Ink	Jumping Jim	Kicking King	Lucy Lamp Lady	Munching Mike

Naughty Nick	Oscar Orange	Poor Peter	Quarrelsome Queen	Robber Red	Sammy Snake	Ticking Tess

Uppy Umbrella	Vase of Violets	Wicked Water Witch	Max and Maxine	Yo-yo Man	Zig Zag Zebra